drums

ACKNOWLEDGEMENTS

Thanks to the following for their help and support: Louise King, Pat Reid, James Cumpsty, Jordan Mclachlan and Kevin Lowery at *Rhythm* magazine; Pete Riley for the recommendation; Joe Walker for being the testing ground; Mike Westergaard for recording the CD; Jim Mathews for guitars on the CD; Iain MacGregor and Chris Harvey at Sanctuary; Claire, Jessie, Joe and Maddie Walker for being drumtastic; Meinl Percussion; Zildjian Cymbals.

This book is for Joe Walker and all the other drumsters starting out on the rhythm of life – have fun with the drum everyone, and it won't be long before you're all great sounding, hard pounding, ground shaking, beat making, cool looking, groove cooking, long lasting, sound blasting, trend setting, go-getting drummers!

Printed in the United Kingdom by
MPG Books Ltd, Bodmin

Published by SMT, an imprint of
Sanctuary Publishing Limited
Sanctuary House
45–53 Sinclair Road
London W14 0NS
United Kingdom

www.sanctuarypublishing.com

Picture Credits: Rex Features,
Redferns and James Cumpsty
Design and Editorial: Essential Works

ISBN: 1-84492-019-4

XTREME

drums

Mark Walker

smt

CONTENTS

INTRODUCTION

Welcome to *Xtreme Drums*, the book that's going to tell you all you need to know about drums and how to play them. With step-by-step lessons you'll soon be playing beats along to your favourite CDs, finding out about some of the greatest drummers in the world and even learning how to play like them...

MEET YOUR TUTOR

Skins is the man who's going to take you through this book, telling you all he knows about the drums and teaching you his favourite beats to play on them. But don't think of him as a tutor – don't even think of him as a friend. Just think of him as a dude, because that's what he is! So let's meet the dude himself...

SKINS IS HERE TO GUIDE YOU...

'Yo! I'm Skins, the guide inside, givin' pride to the ride
Takin' the beat to the street
Makin' it neat, givin' it heat
Makin' it real, givin' it feel, massive appeal...

Aw that's enough. Sorry about that, just remembering my last gig, with a New York rapper. I'm Skins by the way, and I'm going to be taking you through this book you're reading, turning you into a great drummer along the way.'

ADVISE YOU...

'I've played in all sorts of bands – rock, punk, garage, metal, R&B, pop, all sorts. And do you know what? Whatever the style, I always used the same kind of beats – the beats I'm going to teach you in this here book – beats to make you dance, beats to make you groove, beats that might even make your bowels move – Xtreme beats, for Xtreme dudes and dudettes like you...'

TEST YOU...

'Well, I'm sorry about this – we are here to learn something, don't you know? But check this out, the thing we're learning is so cool – drums rule – it's nothing like skool, so having a test to check you're the best is part of the quest – it's a real drum fest.'

MAKE YOU LAUGH...

'I've been playing drums as long as I can remember (and that's a mighty long time), and let me tell you, I love them as much now as I did that Christmas all those years ago when my mum and dad bought me my first drum set. Of course, I liked them even more after the next Christmas when they bought me my first drum sticks... boom boom!'

YOUR DRUM KIT

So you've got a kit that you wanna hit, but you don't know much about it! Well, dudes and dudettes, here's what all the bits on the kit you sit and hit are called…

And the sticks you use to hit the drums are called **DRUM STICKS** – duh!

STOOL What you park your b-u-m on when you're playing.

RIDE CYMBAL The cymbal you sometimes ride (play a rhythm on) instead of the hi-hat.

FLOOR TOM-TOM The larger tom-tom drum that has its own legs so that it can stand alone on the floor. Mounted tom-toms are smaller and attached onto the bass drum.

STANDS All the long metal poles the drums are mounted on are called stands, and each stand is named after the thing that it holds (eg a cymbal stand holds the snare drum – just kidding – the cymbal stand does, of course, hold the cymbal).

BASS DRUM The big drum at the front played with your right foot by kicking a pedal, which is why it's sometimes called the kick drum.

BASS DRUM PEDAL Er, the pedal you use to play the bass drum – boom boom!

DRUM STORY

Most people play the drums
right-handed, but if you are left-
handed you can set the drums
up the other way round, with the
drums and cymbals on the
opposite side. Famous
drummers who play left-handed
include Ian Paice from Deep
Purple and Phil Collins from the
Phil Collins band!

CRASH CYMBAL The cymbal
you crash every now and
again during a song.

HI-HAT CYMBALS These are a
pair of cymbals that you can
play with your sticks or 'chip'
together with your left foot by
pressing the hi-hat pedal, or
even do both at the same time
(phew), which gives a sizzly
kind of sound.

DRUM SKIN The part of the
drum you hit, also called the
'drum head'.

SNARE DRUM Probably the most important drum, and not just because
it's the loudest (though that makes it important in my book, and this is
my book!). The 'snares' are the wires at the bottom of the drum that you
can flick on and off with the switch to change the sound of the drum.
Most of the time the snares are 'on'.

LESSONS

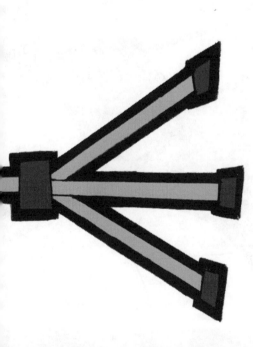

ARE YOU SITTING COMFORTABLY...?

Now I know that you've got the book, you've got your drums and you've got a real strong urge to make some noise, but before we can do that, we need to think about how we're sitting, how we're holding our drum sticks, and how we get ready to play. Because we want to feel swell, ring like a bell, get funky as well – but we don't want to smell. So let's give it some stick... boom boom!

YOUR GOALS

GOAL 1
To sit at the kit correctly, so you can reach all the drums and cymbals.

GOAL 2
To hold the sticks in a relaxed way.

GOAL 3
To play the drums safely.

GOAL 4
To strike the drums properly and make some real good music.

THEORY

In order to play drums you've got to feel good with the wood – that's understood. You've got to start by giving it heart, looking the part, not like some old… you know what I'm saying? Your body has to go with the flow nice and slow, from head to toe. And to do that you have to be ready to drum, and you have to feel comfortable when you play. Here's how…

PROBLEM?

You might find when you first play your arms start aching. To avoid this don't tense them up. Loosen your wrists and don't grip the stick too tightly… but if you do ache, take a break, and after five minutes try again, and next time take it easy drumster!

IN PRACTICE

We're going to start by looking at how to play our drums…

STEP 1

SITTING POSITION. Well, the most important thing here is to sit on the drum stool with your back straight, put your right foot on the bass drum pedal, left foot on the hi-hat pedal, and reach for the stars – well, the drums and cymbals at least.

STEP 2

SAFETY. Before you start to play you should warm up – drumming is a physical activity and your muscles need to be loosened up, so shrug your shoulders, stretch your arms up and down (like you've just scored a goal) and bend your wrists. It's also loud, so you should protect your ears by putting some ear plugs in.

STEP 3

STICK GRIP. There are several ways a drum stick can be held, but for now we'll stick with (get it?) the simplest approach. The stick has two ends: the bead (or tip) and the butt. The bead end is what strikes the drums, and the butt end is the end you hold – yes, yes, you can stop laughing now, butt end, very funny! Don't hold the stick right at the end – it's best to hold it a third of the way up – between the thumb and the forefinger, with the other fingers curled underneath around the stick. Plus you should have the hands slightly turned, so that when you look at them with the stick you can't see the butt end (yes, yes, that's enough about butts – I won't mention them again).

STEP 4

STICK MOVEMENT. Most of the movement of a drum stick comes from the wrist, not the arms, and the stick-swivelling between the fingers, so that when you strike a drum it doesn't make you ache. When you hit the drum, you should flick your wrist and let the stick bounce off the skin – a bit like you would bounce off a trampoline – don't hold it down on the drum.

TIP

Have a good time all of the time! You've bought your drums to make music and have fun, and you should always remember that, even when you're finding it hard. As you go through the book, if you can't play something, don't worry, do something else and try again later – drumming should never be a pain!

EXERCISE

1 STRIKING THE DRUMS Play the parts of your kit in turn, hitting each drum or cymbal four times with each hand before moving onto the next one.

2 HAND TO HAND Now try hitting any drum you fancy, with your hands alternating, going 'right, left, right, left, right, left, etc' – just make some noise and have some fun!

3 WE WILL ROCK YOU The time has come to play a beat, and there's none more famous than the one that goes 'buf buf ka… buf buf ka'. Kick the bass drum twice followed by the snare drum once and you'll have the neighbourhood rocking.

4 SSSHHH! Finally, to stay popular with the people in your house, it's worth practising hitting the drums gently some of the time, or at least not as hard as you possibly can! This will also help you play for longer and become a better drummer as you go along. It's not all about noise (though I admit that is the best bit!).

TEST

QUESTION 1
Where should your feet be when you sit at a drum kit?

QUESTION 2
How should you hold a drum stick?

QUESTION 3
Which parts of the body should you warm up before you drum?

QUESTION 4
Why should you wear ear plugs to play the drums?

HOW TO READ DRUM MUSIC

Buf bam blap, blaba dada bish, buf ka buf ka, pish pish pish.
What am I talking about? Have I, the great Skins, finally lost it?
Of course not – these are just words I use to speak rhythms.
And in this lesson we're going to be learning all about rhythms,
and, more importantly, how to read rhythms… so let's roll!

YOUR GOALS

GOAL 1
To be able to read drum music.

GOAL 2
To understand that each part of the drum kit we play has its own line when written in music.

GOAL 3
To learn the names of the musical notes we use to write out rhythms, and to understand what they mean.

GOAL 4
And most important of all, not to be scared – it's easy once you get the hang of it, honest…

THEORY

Music is written on five lines, known as a stave. In drum music, each line or space between the lines is used for a different part of the drum kit.

Music is broken up into sections called bars, divided on the stave by bar lines. In drum music, bars are often repeated – that means played again and again.

Musical notes have different values of length, and each note has its own name. In drum music the length of the note relates to how quickly the next strike comes.

All music has a 'time signature' at the beginning of it, which tells you how many notes there are in a bar. We don't need to worry too much about this, because in this book all the rhythms will be written in the time signature 4/4, which basically means there will be four counts to a bar.

IN PRACTICE

In the exercises for this lesson we'll be looking at musical notes, how they're written, what they mean and how to start using them.

STEP 1

THE NOTES Notes are figures we use to read and make music, a bit like letters of the alphabet. When we put letters together we get a word, when we put notes together we get music. These are the notes and what they look like:

A crotchet: ♩   A quaver: ♪   A semi-quaver: ♬

To help understand the value or length of the notes, you'll see in the exercises that underneath them are the numbers 1 to 4. There are 4 crotchets, 8 quavers and 16 semi-quavers in a bar.

STEP 2

WHERE THEY GO The next thing we need to know is where each instrument goes on the stave. Let's start with the basics, what I call the meat and potatoes of our kit. The bass drum is written in the bottom space, the snare drum in the second space from the top, the hi-hat when pressed with the foot on the pedal is written on the bottom line, and the hi-hat when struck by the stick is written in the top space above the snare drum.

STEP 3

RESTS AND REPEATS Sometimes when we're drumming what we leave out is as important as what we put in. When reading music we call the notes we leave out 'rests' and rests are written as squiggles. Also, when reading drum music we often repeat bars with the same beat – the repeat sign is two lines and two dots.

STEP 4

COUNTING OUT LOUD When you first read music it helps if you count the time or beat out loud. In 4/4 time each bar has four beats, so counting out loud means saying '1,2,3,4,1,2,3,4, etc' evenly while you're playing. For the crotchets you strike the drum once for each number. For the quavers there is also a note you strike in-between each number – say '1 and 2 and 3 and 4 and, **etc**' while you play. Finally the semi-quavers have three notes between each count – that's the 'uh-and-uh' that you see written under the exercise – try saying the '1 uh-and-uh 2, etc' when you're first playing.

EXERCISE

1 THE NOTES When quavers and semi-quavers are written in groups, the tails at the top of them are joined together as you can see…

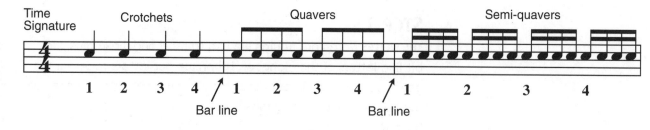

Time Signature   Crotchets   Quavers   Semi-quavers

1   2   3   4   1   2   3   4   1   2   3   4

Bar line   Bar line

2 WHERE THEY GO Each instrument has its own place on the stave. To make things easier hi-hats are written with x's instead of o's, as you can see here…

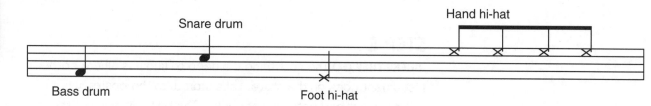

Snare drum   Hand hi-hat

Bass drum   Foot hi-hat

PROBLEM?

When you come to play Exercise 4 the semi-quavers will be quite hard. Try repeating each bar four times before moving onto the next one, and don't start the crotchets too fast, or you won't be able to play the semi-quavers without your hands exploding – uuuugh!

3. RESTS AND REPEATS

Crotchet rest	Quaver rest	Semi-quaver rest	Repeat bar

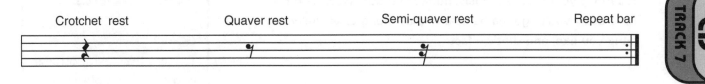

4. COUNTING OUT LOUD When you play these patterns on any of your drums play with both hands, going 'right, left, right, left, right, left…'

1   2   3   4   1 & 2 & 3 & 4 &   1 uh & uh 2 uh & uh 3 uh & uh 4 uh & uh

TEST

QUESTION 1
What are the lines that music is written on called?

QUESTION 2
What space is the bass drum written on?

QUESTION 3
How many crotchets are there in a 4/4 bar?

QUESTION 4
Which is quicker – four crotchets or four quavers?

TIP

You can practice the idea of counting out loud by counting along to your favourite songs, whether it's pop, rap, house, R&B, garage, rock, punk, or nursery rhymes. Listen to the music and count '1, 2, 3 ,4' over and over with the beat.

THE BASIC BEAT

Lesson 3 is a real treat, it's the basic beat, it's really neat, and it'll move your feet. Seriously, dudes and dudettes, with this little baby you're gonna be able to play along to virtually any song you like, and that's a fact.

THEORY

This is where we begin to get down to it drumsters. If we work hard at this lesson everything else will fall into place, it'll be just ace, so watch this space, and keep up the pace. Because once you've mastered the basic beat you'll definitely be able to call yourself a drummer. Really concentrate and soon you'll be impressing your friends and family – though probably not your neighbours – they never seem to be fans of the sound of you having a ball coming through their wall! But have no fear, just persevere, the ride starts here…

YOUR GOALS

GOAL 1
To learn the basic patterns and parts (see glossary) that make up a full beat.

GOAL 2
To learn which hand plays which bit of the kit, and where our hands go to do that.

GOAL 3
To understand that each drum we play has its own place within a rhythm.

GOAL 4
To be able to play along to all our favourite songs – blaba dada bif – how cool is that?

IN PRACTICE

In the exercises we'll be looking at what makes up a basic drum beat.
Here's the things to think about when you play...

STEP 1

HI-HAT PATTERN. When you play the hi-hat keep it closed. You can
do this by keeping your left foot down, or even clamp it that way.
Strike the top hi-hat cymbal with the tip of the stick, between the
edge and the bell (the raised bit in the middle of the cymbal).

STEP 2

BASS DRUM PART. Here comes the first decision you've got to
make for yourselves drumsters – how you put your foot on the
pedal. Basically, you can have your whole foot on the bass drum
pedal, with your heel touching the bottom, or you can just have
your toe near the top with the rest of your foot in the air. Right
now, do whatever is most comfortable for you.

STEP 3

SNARE DRUM PART. Strike the snare drum in the middle, and
remember, don't hold the stick down onto the skin – let it bounce
off, and hold it up ready for the next beat.

STEP 4

THE BEAT. This is hard, but to help you put all three bits together,
try practising just two at a time – start with the bass drum and
the snare drum. If you count '1, 2, 3, 4' while you play, the bass
drum should go on the '1' and '3' and the snare drum on the '2'
and '4'. Next try just the snare and the hi-hat, and then the bass
drum and the hi-hat. Then put them all together and what have
you got? You've got the lot! Go on, give it some stick...

PROBLEM?

To make reading easier, the rests are no longer shown when the
different parts are written together for the full beat, and the snare
drum is attached to the hi-hat. This should also make it easier to see
which parts are hit at the same time.

EXERCISE

1 HI-HAT PATTERN Play this with your right hand.

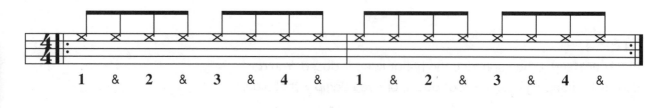

2 BASS DRUM PART Play this with your right foot.

3 SNARE DRUM PART Play this with your left hand.

4 THE BEAT Play this with your right hand on the hi-hat going over your left hand on the snare drum.

TIP

When you play along to the CD wear headphones so you can hear the beats more clearly. And if you can only do it for a few bars, try playing along to other CDs by your favourite band to build up your stamina.

TEST

QUESTION 1
In the basic beat, which parts of the kit do your left and right hands hit?

QUESTION 2
How should you play your bass drum pedal – with your whole foot or just your toe (yes, it is a trick question – duh!)?

QUESTION 3
What are patterns and parts (and we're not talking knitting or models here)?

QUESTION 4
How can you practise the basic beat to help you play for longer?

XTRA BASS DRUM BEATS

Now you've got down and funky with the basic beat, the time has come to turn up the heat. So for this lesson we're going to invest, digest and progress by taking the basic beat and adding extra parts to the bass drum pattern. Can you kick it? Yes you can…

YOUR GOALS

GOAL 1
To learn a new bass drum part to go with the basic beat snare and hi-hat patterns.

GOAL 2
To understand that some parts we play on the kit can stay the same while other parts change.

GOAL 3
To start feeling comfortable with our bass drum doing more complicated patterns.

GOAL 4
Not to get confused when drum patterns change just a little bit – this sounds easy, but believe me, a slight difference can be really weird sometimes. Like when your granny forgets to put on her make-up – you know what I'm saying…

THEORY

There are two ways of adding an extra bass drum beat, so that instead of going 'buf', we go 'buf buf'! And it's really worth working on this, because you know in Lesson 3 when I said the basic beat can accompany any song? Well, that's true – as if I, your mate Skins, would lie to you! But, if you listen carefully to the drums on a track, you'll hear that most songs have slightly different beats. The snare is virtually always the backbeat (see glossary), falling on the '2' and '4' count, but the bass drum can vary quite a lot.

IN PRACTICE

Okay drumsters, here's what you need to think about when you start to play the exercises…

STEP 1

HI-HAT PATTERN Same as before I'm afraid, though if you want to make a change when practising it on its own, try playing it on the bell and the edge

STEP 2

BASS DRUM PART The two bars are slightly different. If you count '1 and 2 and 3 and 4 and' you'll see that in the first bar the single bass drum falls on the '1', then there's a gap and then the double beat falls on the '3 and'. But in the second bar, although the single beat is the same, the double beat starts earlier, on the 'and 3'.

STEP 3

SNARE DRUM PART Same as before, snore, snore, snore, snore…
But you know what they say – practice makes perfect. What do
you mean 'who's they'? 'They' is obviously anyone who's a
perfectionist I'd imagine.

STEP 4

THE XTRA BASS DRUM BEAT As with the basic beat, try doing just
the bass drum and snare drum before adding the hi-hat, and also
the hi-hat and bass drum together. That way you'll be good and
ready when it comes to playing the beat, the whole beat and
nothing but the beat.

PROBLEM?

If your foot can't play the two bass drum beats quick enough, slow down – duh! It's not a race, so set a pace that's not in your face like you're being chased, but it's on the case in a comfortable place without too much haste – mmmm, that's ace!

EXERCISE

CD TRACK 13

1 HI-HAT PATTERN Play with your right hand.

CD TRACK 14

2 BASS DRUM PART Play with your right foot.

CD TRACK 15

3 SNARE DRUM PART Play this part, known as the backbeat, with your left hand.

CD TRACK 16

4 THE BEAT Play all the patterns together, with your right hand on the hi-hat going over your left hand on the snare drum.

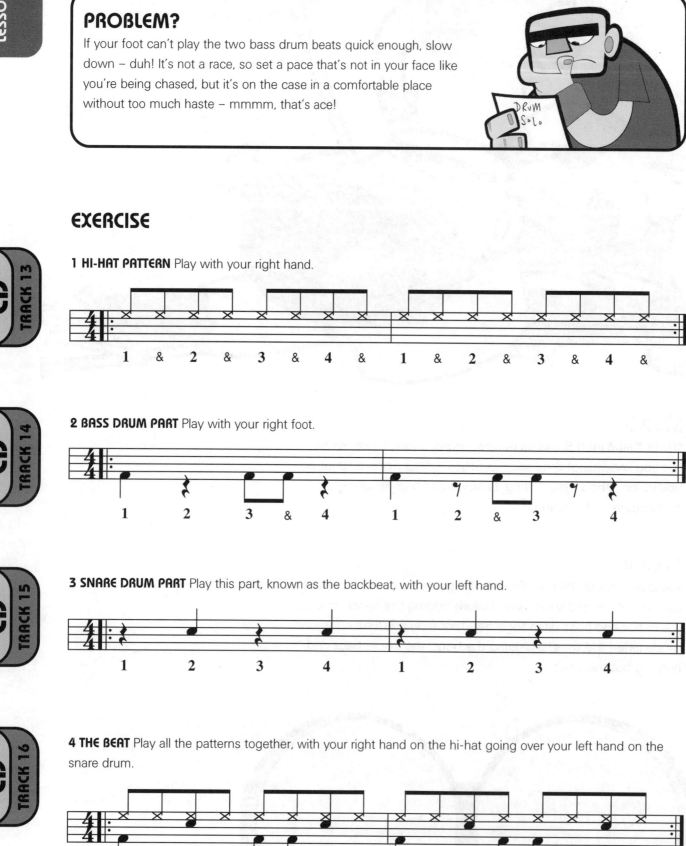

TEST

QUESTION 1
What is the name given to a beat with the '2' and '4' on the snare drum?

QUESTION 2
How many ways do we play the two bass drum strikes in this lesson?

QUESTION 3
What do you need to do if your foot can't play the two bass drum strikes quickly enough?

QUESTION 4
What's the similarity between drum beats and your granny's make-up?

XTRA SNARE DRUM BEATS

For Lesson 5 we're going to mess with the basic beat again, but this time it's the single snare we'll turn into a pair, doubling up every other beat to make a groove so sweet it's perfectly neat. And just to bring a freshness to the playing, we'll use our ride cymbal instead of the hi-hat. I sure am a radical dude…

YOUR GOALS

GOAL 1
To learn a new snare drum part to go with the basic beat, bass drum and hi-hat patterns.

GOAL 2
To understand that changing just a little bit of a beat can make a big difference to the sound and help make the drums more interesting.

GOAL 3
To add new sounds to your beats by using the cymbals and tom-tom instead of the hi-hats.

GOAL 4
To start making up your own beats – once you've finished this lesson you can start to pick'n'mix your favourite parts and patterns from Lessons 3, 4 and 5.

THEORY

Now my little drumsters, as we get further into this book we're going to be doing little things that change the sound of what we do quite radically. As I said in Lesson 3, you can play the basic beat to virtually anything, and the basic beat is the building block from which we make all drum grooves (see glossary). But what makes drums really interesting are the bits we add to the basic beat. In this lesson we're going to change the snare drum – it will still be a backbeat, we're just going to make it a more interesting backbeat – a pat on the back-beat…boom boom!

IN PRACTICE

When we play the exercises for this lesson we're going to start making some changes to what our hands are doing…

STEP 1

RIDE CYMBAL PATTERN When you first hit the ride cymbal try hitting it in the middle between the edge and the bell. This is where you should get the 'sweetest' sound. Then you can try playing on the bell which makes a clunkier chiming sound.

STEP 2

BASS DRUM PART Back to the basic bass drum part from the basic beat, so you shouldn't need too much practice by now…

STEP 3

SNARE DRUM PART Here's that extra beat. If you're counting '1 and 2 and 3 and 4 and' the first snare hit is the usual backbeat, a single strike on the '2', but the second one is different, with an added stroke that comes after the '4', so you hit the drum twice on '4 and'.

STEP 4

THE BEAT This is where we put it all together. Once you've got this down, you can start to make up your own beats by pick'n'mixing from all the lessons so far, interchanging the bass and snare drum parts, and using different bits of your kit. You could even get a really tribal-sounding beat by playing the backbeat on your mounted tom and the right hand on your floor tom. The world, as they say, is your oyster. Who's 'they'? Someone who loves oysters I'd imagine.

> **TIP**
> The ride cymbal is usually placed on your right-hand side, so you don't need to cross your hands for this one – drumtastic! And if you don't have a ride cymbal use your crash cymbal instead, or just play the floor tom-tom.

PROBLEM?

The floor tom may sound loud and boomy. Try sticking a duster or piece of cloth to the skin near the edge. This is called dampening, and makes the drum give more of a thud than a boom sound – 'duf' rather than 'boingngngngngng...'

EXERCISE

1 RIDE CYMBAL PATTERN Play with your right hand on the cymbal or floor tom.

2 BASS DRUM PART As always, play with your right foot.

3 SNARE DRUM PART Play this part with your left hand.

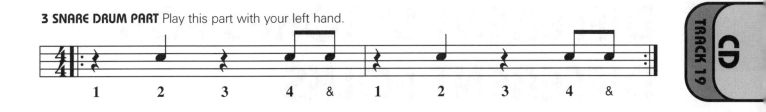

TRACK 19

4 THE BEAT Play all the patterns together, with your right hand on the cymbal or tom-tom.

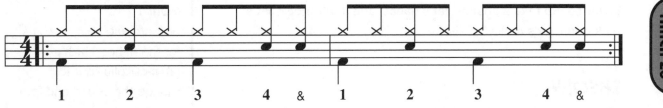

TRACK 20

TEST

QUESTION 1
Where should you hit the cymbal?

QUESTION 2
Is a double snare beat still a backbeat?

QUESTION 3
What kind of beat does it sound like when you play the toms instead of the cymbals?

QUESTION 4
How many different beats can you make by pick'n'mixing different parts and patterns from the last three lessons?

DIFFERENT STROKES FOR DIFFERENT FOLKS

Okay my drum chums, this is where we start to take a look at new ways to play our drums for different styles, namely rock and dance, two of the most popular types of music ever invented. So take a chance, let's dance, and don't mock, let's rock dude, let's rock…

THEORY

Up until now we've always played quavers on the hi-hat or cymbal with our right hand, whatever the beat. Well now, that's about to change, and it may seem strange, and somewhat deranged, but it's well within our range – by using crotchets and semi-quavers instead of the traditional quavers we can completely alter the feel of the rhythms we make, and start to play different styles of music. So once we've learned these we'll be able to dance the night away and go rockin' all over the world. I like it, I like it, I la-la-like it. Here we go….

IN PRACTICE

In these exercises we're going to start looking at different hi-hat patterns, what's known as 4s and 16s (8s are what we've been doing up until now). 4s, 8s and 16s are expressions we use to describe what we play on the hi-hat. 4s are basically crotchets, 8s are quavers, and 16s are semi-quavers. Hi-hat, hi-hat, it's off to work we strut…

STEP 1

4s HI-HAT PATTERN This will give us a good rock beat. To get an authentic 'rock' sound try hitting the hi-hat on the edge of the cymbals with the top shaft of the stick – ie not the bead but just below the bead. To help do this try dropping your right elbow a bit lower than you usually have it, and don't have your foot pressed quite as tightly on the hi-hat pedal.

STEP 2

16s HI-HAT PATTERN I'm afraid this one is more tricky my little drumsters. You basically need to play this in a manner that we drummers like to call 'hand to hand'. This means you hit the hi-hats with alternating strokes, going 'right, left, right, left, right, left, etc' (a bit like marching but much cooler)! And to make it sound good we need to hit on the top of the hi-hat with the beads of our sticks.

STEP 3

4s BEAT – ROCK Play this as it's written, so basically the hi-hat is only hit when a snare drum or bass drum is hit, on the '1, 2, 3, 4'. For heavy rock do it quite slowly, and for punk rock try it twice the speed…

STEP 4

16s BEAT – DANCE This is the hardest thing yet. When doing 16s both hands are playing the hi-hat – 'right, left, right, left, etc'. But when you hit the snare drum on the '2' and the '4' (our good old friend the backbeat), your right hand comes off the hi-hat to strike the snare, so for that strike the hi-hat is not hit…!!!

PROBLEM?

Your hands may get in a muddle when you first play the 16s beat. Go back to just playing the hi-hat whilst counting '1, 2, 3, 4' and when you're comfortable bring your right hand onto the snare drum for the '2' and the '4'.

EXERCISE

CD TRACK 21

1 4S HI-HAT PATTERN Right hand on hi-hat.

1   2   3   4   1   2   3   4

CD TRACK 22

2 16S HI-HAT PATTERN Right and left hand alternating on hi-hat.

1 uh & uh 2 uh & uh 3 uh & uh 4 uh & uh   1 uh & uh 2 uh & uh 3 uh & uh 4 uh & uh

3 4S BEAT – ROCK

1   2   3   4   1   2   3 & 4

TRACK 23 · CD

4 16S BEAT – DANCE

1   2   3   4   1   2   3   4

TRACK 24 · CD

TIP

Start practising the 16s beat nice and slowly. It'll sound like mush indeed, if you rush without need, but if you crush the speed, it'll sound lush – guaranteed!

TEST

QUESTION 1
What do we call a beat playing crotchets on the hi-hat?

QUESTION 2
What do we call a beat playing semi-quavers on the hi-hat?

QUESTION 3
What type of rock do we use a fast 4s beat for?

QUESTION 4
When we play a 16s beat, do we hit the snare drum with the left hand or the right hand?

OPENING AND CLOSING THE HI-HATS

Well, here we go drumsters, at last we're going to find out the answer to that six-million-drummer question that's been nagging you for a while now – no, not the one about Britney and Madonna – the question in question is when do we get to use our left foot? And the answer is …NOW! Get down and get with it, drumsters!

YOUR GOALS

GOAL 1
To stop using three limbs and start using four – that's right, your left foot is going to have to start moving too for the top hi-hat cymbal to move up and down…

GOAL 2
To learn what it means to describe a hi-hat as being 'open' and 'closed'.

GOAL 3
To add new sounds to our collection by playing the hi-hat when it is 'open'.

GOAL 4
To work on our co-ordination (see glossary) between our left and right feet, because they will need to move up and down at different times.

THEORY

Well, my masters of the beat generation, this is the time to sort out the men from the boys, the ladies from the girls, and the straight hairs from the curls. Because this is the first time we have to use not one, not two, not three, but four – yes, I said four – limbs. Both hands and both feet… at the same time! 'Zoiks,' I hear you say (or something a bit ruder). But this is what you need next to progress in the quest to be best in the west (or north, south and east).

IN PRACTICE

In this lesson we'll be using 'open' and 'closed' hi-hats. Basically, the words 'open' and 'closed' mean exactly what they say (hooray!). When the cymbals are apart they are 'open', and when they are pushed together they are 'closed.' It's an open and shut case…

STEP 1

4s HI-HAT WITH FOOT Up until now our left leg has merely been resting to keep the hi-hat down. Well, now it's time to start moving it up and down in a smooooooooth action. It's easiest if you keep your whole foot on the pedal (heel and toe) and just lift your toe to move the top cymbal up and down.

STEP 2

BASS DRUM AND HI-HAT WITH FOOT This should help you start getting your co-ordination together, with the right and left feet alternating – taking it in turns to go up and down, a bit like a see-saw, closing the hi-hat on the '2' and '4': our old friend the backbeat. When we play the exercise properly we get that classic drum rhythm 'boom chick boom chick boom chick boom chick…' – bootiful.

STEP 3

HI-HAT WITH HAND AND FOOT When you open the hi-hat with your foot while playing the quavers on it with your stick, try opening it as you strike it on the 'and' before the '2' and the '4'. Then close it as you play the next strike, so it clicks back down on the '2' and the '4'. That way you should get a good clean sound.

STEP 4

FULL BEAT WITH OPENING HI-HAT When you play the full beat, notice that the hi-hat clicks down on the same beat as the snare, and becomes part of the backbeat. For this to really work and sound good, we've got to make sure we open the hi-hat 'cleanly', in other words as the stick strikes it on the note before.

PROBLEM?

To help us know when to open the hi-hat in the right place we put a little 'umbrella' above the hi-hat music to show the strike we open it on. To get the idea of how the opening and closing hi-hat should sound listen to the CD before you play it!

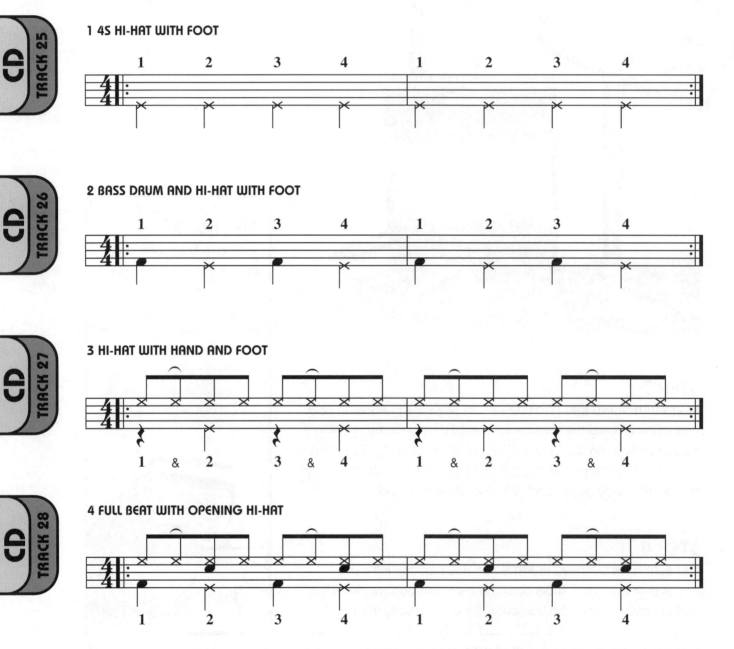

TIP

If you can't do it then give up... no, no, no, I'm only joking!
Never give up on a good thing. It's as simple as this – if at first
you don't succeed, drum, drum and drum again. Er, and maybe
try slowing down...

EXERCISE

1 4S HI-HAT WITH FOOT

TRACK 25

2 BASS DRUM AND HI-HAT WITH FOOT

TRACK 26

3 HI-HAT WITH HAND AND FOOT

TRACK 27

4 FULL BEAT WITH OPENING HI-HAT

TRACK 28

TEST

QUESTION 1
What's the difference between an open and closed hi-hat?

QUESTION 2
How can we get a classic 'boom chick boom chick' rhythm?

QUESTION 3
On which strike of the beat do we open the hi-hat when we're playing quavers on it with our stick?

QUESTION 4
Don't you just love drums?

FILL-INS, RUDIMENTS AND ACCENTS

Now before we go any further, the first thing to straighten out is that this is NOT a lesson about fruit jams for your cakes, immensely rude men or speaking like the French. It is in fact about some completely new concepts that will take you onto the next level of playing. Are you sticking comfortably? Then we'll begin...

THEORY

A fill-in is basically a break in a beat, something we can use to take us into another section of a song, like going from a verse to a chorus. We won't actually be learning much about how we use fill-ins in this lesson, we'll just be learning about the rudiments that we can use to play fill-ins. Sound complicated? Have no fear, all will become clear – though it might take a year! With drums, a rudiment is basically a type of pattern played with the sticks. And when we play a rudiment some strokes are played harder than others – these are called accents. I think we'd better move on, don't you...?

IN PRACTICE

Each of the patterns in the exercises is a drum rudiment. Rudiments are normally practised on the snare drum, and involve co-ordinated movements between the hands. You'll notice that above each note in the exercises the letters 'R' and 'L' appear. These basically mean 'right' and 'left' and tell us which hand strikes the drum – what we call sticking (see glossary).

STEP 1

SINGLE-STROKE ROLL This is probably the easiest rudiment, and is also the one most used for fill-ins. The sticking is what we call 'hand to hand', and is regular. It's probably easiest if you repeat each bar on its own several times before doubling up the speed for the next bar – eg when you go from crotchets to quavers.

STEP 2

DOUBLE-STROKE ROLL This is probably the hardest rudiment, at least it is once you start 'bouncing' your stick. Look at the sticking 'RRLLRRLL' and for now concentrate primarily on the first two bars, playing each one four times before going to the next one. Don't worry too much about the semi-quavers – you have to bounce the stick on the skin to play it at speed, and it takes forever to perfect. I've been trying to get it right since I was a youngster, and that's a mighty long time.

STEP 3

PARADIDDLE Here you see your first accents. The sign > above a note means you have to accent that note, in other words strike it harder. To play a paradiddle you basically play two single strokes, followed by a double stroke, followed by two singles, followed by a double and so on, and the accent comes after each double.

STEP 4

THREE-STROKE RUFF For the three-stroke ruff the sticking is alternate – right, left, right, left, etc – but there is a gap after every three notes. The accent comes on the last note before the gap. You can vary this if you want by putting the accent on the first note after the gap. Thank you? No worries, I'm feeling generous.

PROBLEM?

You may find concentrating on accents and sticking for the paradiddle and ruff hard to do. Don't worry, try getting the sticking right first (ie which hand is playing when) before you worry about putting the accents in. And try playing them on the tom-toms as well as the snare drum.

TIP

The great thing about rudiments is you can practise them anywhere to learn the co-ordination. You don't even need sticks, you can do them with your hands on your lap, on a table, on the back seat of a car, on your desk at school, even just in your head…

EXERCISE

1 SINGLE-STROKE ROLL

R L R L   R L R L R L R L   R L R L R L R L R L R L R L R L

1 2 3 4   1 2 3 4   1   2   3   4

2 DOUBLE-STROKE ROLL

R R L L   R R L L R R L L   R R L L R R L L R R L L R R L L

1 2 3 4   1 2 3 4   1   2   3   4

3 PARADIDDLE

TRACK 31

4 THREE-STROKE RUFF

TRACK 32

TEST

QUESTION 1
What is a rudiment?

QUESTION 2
Can you name four different rudiments?

QUESTION 3
Which rudiment has the sticking RLRR LRLL RLRR LRLL?

QUESTION 4
How can we play the three stroke ruff differently to the way it is written?

BEATS WITH FILL-INS

Here we go, here we go, here we go... (you can sing that bit if you like). Well, this is it my little drumming friends. Now's when we really start to sound like our heroes (and that bloke in the top class at school), because now is the time to start adding things to our beats that will make us sound as flash as cash with a crash and a bash.

YOUR GOALS

GOAL 1
To start using the crash cymbal and tom-toms more often, and learn where on the stave they are written.

GOAL 2
To understand that a fill-in is used at the end of a musical section to take us into the next part of a song.

GOAL 3
To realise that once you've got the hang of the idea of fill-ins, you can make up your own.

GOAL 4
There's no getting away from this one – to make your playing really cool...

THEORY

Fill-ins are one of the best ways that drummers can put their own stamp on a track. When you first listen to the drums in a song, the bits that make you go 'Yo, nice one!' are normally the fills rather than the beats, and all drummers have their own way of doing fills. The exercises here are just examples, but should give you the necessary tools to start making up your own… Incidentally, you generally only play fill-ins at the end of a section of music, so when you play these exercises along to CDs or tapes, do the beat for a while before you play a fill-in – don't play them every other bar like in the exercises – duh!

IN PRACTICE

In exercises 2, 3 and 4 we're going to learn how to add a fill-in to a beat.

STEP 1

TOM-TOMS AND CRASH CYMBAL Exercise 1 will show you where on the stave the new parts of the kit we are using are written, and just as when you learned to read the snare, bass drum and hats, take your time over checking out which bit goes where, though to be honest, as long as you hit a tom it doesn't matter too much which one you hit – a bit like brothers and sisters… boom boom!

STEP 2

SINGLE-STROKE ROLL FILL-IN For the fill-in, the first four semi-quavers are on the snare drum. To start with play the second bar (ie just the fill-in), over and over again to get the feel for what we call rolling round the kit. Then try putting it after the beat.

STEP 3

FUNKY FILL-IN The quavers on the '1' and '3' in the fill-in are played on the snare drum, and the semi-quavers on the toms. But to get used to the pattern of the fill, play it all on the same drum to start with.

STEP 4

ROCKIN' FILL-IN By using three-stroke ruffs at the start of this fill we break up the flow a bit, which is a nice thing to do when you're playing rock music. Again, practise it on just one drum before you split it up around the kit.

PROBLEM?

When you start it will be hard to get back into the beat after a fill-in, so at first try playing the last bit of the fill (on the '4'), just doing the four semi-quavers that take you back to the beat. Keep doing this until you flow easily into the beat.

EXERCISE

CD TRACK 33

1 TOM-TOMS AND CRASH CYMBAL

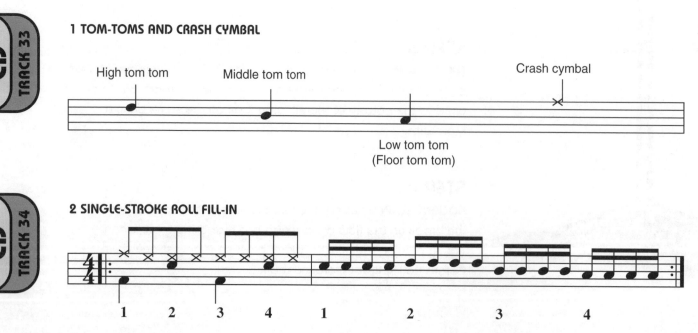

High tom tom   Middle tom tom   Crash cymbal

Low tom tom
(Floor tom tom)

CD TRACK 34

2 SINGLE-STROKE ROLL FILL-IN

3 FUNKY FILL-IN

TRACK 35

4 ROCKIN' FILL-IN

TRACK 36

TIP

Notice how in the music the first strike of bar one is a crash cymbal. At the end of a fill-in it is usual to hit the crash cymbal along with the bass drum on the first beat of the next bar – listen to the CD to hear this.

TEST

QUESTION 1
On which space of the stave do you find the low tom-tom (floor tom)?

QUESTION 2
What do you hit on the first beat of the bar after a fill-in?

QUESTION 3
Would you normally do a fill-in after every beat?

QUESTION 4
What's the similarity between tom-toms and brothers and sisters?

GRACE NOTES

I can't believe it. This is the last lesson. And it feels like we only just met. Well, if you've got this far, you're a bit of a star, you've jumped the bar, hip hip hurrah! And the next thing to say is… CONGRATULATIONS drumster! You are obviously now a real top drummer, and with this lesson under your belt you'll rule the world for sure!

YOUR GOALS

GOAL 1
To learn about and work on dynamics (see glossary) by adding parts to our beats that are played quietly.

GOAL 2
To make our co-ordination even better.

GOAL 3
To add to our understanding that although drums generally just play a backbeat in music, there are many different ways we can create that backbeat.

GOAL 4
To learn to play grace notes with grace.

THEORY

A drummer's role (as opposed to roll) in a band is to provide the backbeat to the songs we play. As we discovered right at the beginning in Lesson 3, with the basic beat we can play along to any song. But sometimes we need something a bit more interesting to make the music more lively, what we call 'feel good'. Adding bass drums, changing the hi-hat pattern, playing on the ride cymbal and playing fill-ins all do this. And so does adding 'grace notes' – these are quieter strikes on our snare drum that are played in-between the '2' and '4' backbeat. Some drummers call them ghost notes. They're basically exactly the same, though ghost notes are a little scarier… boom boom! Anyway, let's get on our drums real quick, be slick, and let's kick a new lick with our latest trick – give it some stick!

IN PRACTICE

The co-ordination needed to play grace notes is complicated, so this lesson takes us through it step by step…

STEP 1

HI-HAT AND SNARE DRUM CONCEPT Grace notes are played on the snare drum in-between the hi-hat 8s part. To get used to the idea, Exercise 1 is basically a single-stroke roll between the hi-hat and snare, with the right hand on the hi-hat and the left hand on the snare.

STEP 2

HI-HAT PLUS SNARE DRUM GRACE NOTES Next we take some of the snare beats out. If you count '1 uh-and-uh 2 uh-and-uh 3 uh-and-uh 4 uh-and-uh' the snare grace notes are basically the 'uh' immediately before and after the '3'. This is hard to read, so listen carefully to the CD and try playing along with that.

STEP 3

HI-HAT SNARE DRUM GRACE NOTES AND BACKBEAT And then we put the backbeat in – as you will see, the grace notes go between the '2' and '4' strike of the backbeat. Don't worry too much about the accents at first. Concentrate on getting the sticking right, then bring the volume of the grace notes down.

STEP 4

FULL BEAT And to make our beat complete so we can take it to the street, we'll add a double bass drum. The grace notes basically go just before each of the second lot of bass drums in each bar. So it sounds something like this – 'buf buf kah, ka bu ka bu kah, buf buf kah, ka bu ka bu kah'. Now that's what I call a groove – groovetastic!

PROBLEM?

You'll probably be a bit sad that this is the last lesson – I know I am. Don't worry, you can put your tissues away – if you go to the 'In The Style Of…' section, you'll find lots of new ways to play a few of your favourite things… hurrah!

CD TRACK 37

CD TRACK 38

CD TRACK 39

CD TRACK 40

EXERCISE

1 HI-HAT AND SNARE DRUM CONCEPT

2 HI-HAT PLUS SNARE DRUM GRACE NOTES

3 HI-HAT PLUS SNARE DRUM GRACE NOTES AND BACKBEAT

4 FULL BEAT

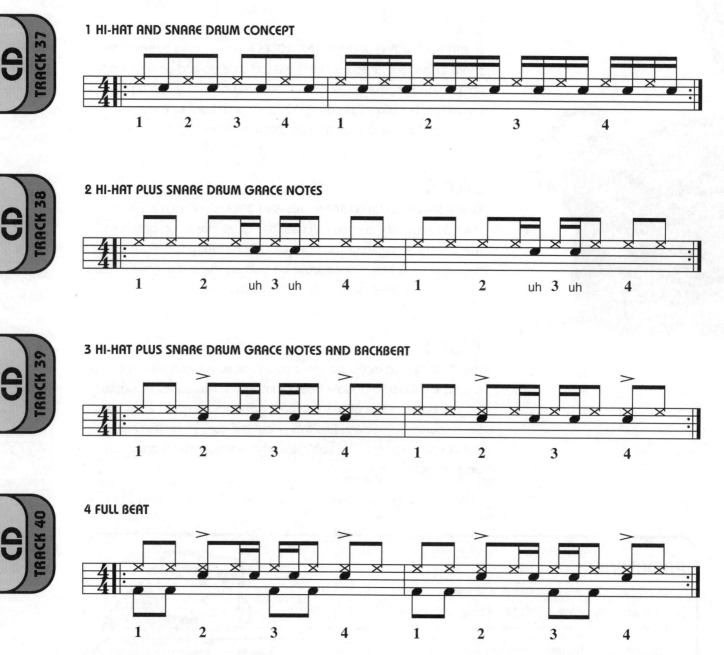

TEST

QUESTION 1
Which rudiment is used to play Exercise 1?

QUESTION 2
What are grace notes?

QUESTION 3
Which famous beat do you get if you play the full beat in this lesson without the grace notes?

QUESTION 4
This is the final question, and it's an important one – did you make that smell?

TOP 10 ARTISTS

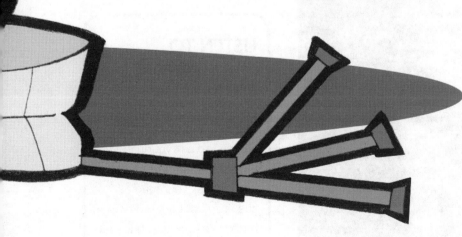

TRACK 41

CHARLIE WATTS

It's Charlie Watts – what's he got? He's got the lot! Renowned as the sharpest dressed drummer in the biz, Charlie is rarely seen without a suit and tie – a true gent. Massive respect is due and given to Mr Watts – he's been playing with The Rolling Stones, (also known as 'the greatest rock 'n' roll band in the world') for over 40 years, and in that time has been the backbone of the band. His first love was jazz music, and he was a graphic designer by profession, but when the blues exploded onto the UK scene in the early '60s Mick Jagger and Keith Richards snapped him up for their new band The Rolling Stones, and the rest, as they say, is history. The Stones still tour the world, and when he's not playing with them he has his own jazz band to play with.

STATISTICS

DATE OF BIRTH
2 July 1941

PLACE OF BIRTH
London, England

INFLUENCES
Fats Domino, Little Richard, Charlie Parker, (jazz saxophonist who Charlie wrote a book about), and jazz drummers Phil Seamen and Kenny Clarke

FIRST HIT
'Time Is On My Side'

HIGHEST CHART POSITION
#1 (about a zillion times all around the world)

INSTRUMENTS USED
Gretsch drums and Zildjian cymbals

LISTEN TO
Any *ROLLING STONES GREATEST HITS* you can get your hands on! They have had loads of greatest hits albums, so ask your dad for one of his, and if he hasn't got any, ask your mum. If she hasn't got any, sorry to have to tell you this, but your folks are a little square…

IN THE STYLE OF...

In the '60s, most of the the Rolling Stones's songs were a party from the word go, and Charlie Watts pushed them along from start to finish. The Stones have had more hits than you can shake a stick at, and Charlie's simple drumming is a key part of their success. The beats he plays to most of their songs are fairly similar – basic beats with simple fill-ins – but as the old saying goes, 'It ain't what you do, it's the way that you do it…' and the way Charlie does it is like no one else.

HOW TO PLAY LIKE CHARLIE WATTS

If you watch Charlie Watts, the first thing you notice is that he doesn't hit his hi-hat when he hits his snare drum. This is because when he first played with the Rolling Stones he couldn't lift his left hand high enough to get a loud backbeat unless he lifted his right hand out of the way. So the first thing to do to sound like Charlie is miss out your hi-hat when you hit your snare drum on the backbeat. In other words the hi-hat goes 'chick chick chick stop chick chick chick stop chick chick chick stop' and so on. His bass drum playing is always quite consistant – once he has a bass drum pattern he keeps it pretty regular throughout. For our example we'll go 'buf buf, buf buf, buf buf' and so on. Then if you add the snare drum on the '2' and '4' of each bar like we've done in the lessons, you basically have the essence of a Charlie Watts beat.

TRUE STORY

Charlie's famous for his quick quips. My favourite was when the Stones were celebrating their 25th anniversary. He was asked what it was like playing with the band for 25 years, and he said 'Five years playing, twenty years hanging around…' Another time Mick Jagger was calling for him and shouted 'Where's my drummer?' To which Charlie answered 'I'm not your drummer, you're my singer!'… boom boom!

DAVE GROHL

He's on a roll, he's the great Dave Grohl! This cat is so cool he not only played drums in the greatest rock band of the '90s – Nirvana – he now plays guitar, sings and writes the songs for the riffingest band of the 21st Century, The Foo Fighters. And he's even drummed for Queens Of The Stone Age too! He's Rock with a great big capital R! Oh, and he's a really nice bloke. In Nirvana he helped change the face and sound of rock music by propelling grunge into the stratosphere – their album *Nevermind*, with its melodic songs and amazing dynamics (really quiet verses, really LOUD choruses), sold millions and millions of copies. And the song 'Smells Like Teen Spirit' has one of the most bombastic drum fills of all time – check out the way Dave thrashes his snare drum to within an inch of its life when the song explodes into the chorus. Now that's what I call music!

LISTEN TO

WITH NIRVANA –
NEVERMIND
'Smells Like Teen Spirit', 'Come As You Are', 'In Bloom'

WITH THE FOO FIGHTERS –
THE COLOUR AND THE SHAPE
'Monkey Wrench', 'My Hero'

STATISTICS

DATE OF BIRTH
14 January 1969

PLACE OF BIRTH
Warren, Ohio, USA

INFLUENCES
Rush, Led Zeppelin, The Bad Brains, The Beatles, Soundgarden

FIRST HIT
'Smells Like Teen Spirit'

HIGHEST CHART POSITION
'Heart Shaped Box' – #5 – 1993 and 'All My Life' – #5 – 2003

INSTRUMENTS USED
Tama drums and Zildjian cymbals

IN THE STYLE OF...

When Nirvana released 'Smells Like Teen Spirit' on the world in 1991 little did they know (or the world for that matter) how they were going to change rock music forever. One of the main ingredients of grunge is dynamics, with sparse quiet verses and full-on loud choruses, and in my book, (and this is my book), Dave Grohl is the master of dynamics.

HOW TO PLAY LIKE DAVE GROHL

Dave's dynamics aren't just playing quietly and loudly. He also does what's called 'build' his parts. This means adding more bass drums to a pattern and opening the hi-hat for bridges and choruses, making it more splashy. We're going to do a basic grunge beat with the hi-hats slightly open and a '2' and '4' backbeat on the snare. To drive a song along Dave often plays quavers on the bass drum between each snare, so that's what we'll do. And to finish it off we'll do the mother of all fill-ins, one of Dave's absolute classics. The bass drum keeps playing 8s while he thrashes 16s on the snare drum stopping with an accent on the '4'.

TRACK 43 CD

TRUE STORY

When Nirvana's singer, Kurt Cobain, died in 1994, drummers were worried Dave might give up forever. Instead, he recorded his own album, *Foo Fighters*, writing the songs, singing them, and playing guitar as well as drums. It was so successful that the Foo Fighters became a band – nowadays Dave is the frontman, playing guitar and doing lead vocals, while another famous drummer, Taylor Hawkins, bashes the tubs behind him. Sometimes at live shows they have two kits set up and Dave and Taylor play together, which always sends the audience wild...

SUPERSTAR TIP

'Drumming is songwriting, it just has to do with the drums being a song within a song.' And what Dave's saying here drumsters is that when you play in a band and make music, the beats you invent are as important as the tune and the words. Without a beat, songs are just boring...

DERRICK McKENZIE

Don't get in a frenzy, it's only Derrick McKenzie, who lays down the funktastic grooves for the funktastic music of the funktastic Jamiroquai. Derrick has been beating away with the band since 1993, and in that time has played on a whole host of hits. What Derrick and Jamiroquai have done with their music is taken the disco beats of the '70s and turned them into dance beats for the '90s and new millennium. Derrick is helped in the grooves by his great friend Sola Akingbola, Jamiroquai's percussionist, and together they make some of the grooviest beats you'll ever hear.

LISTEN TO

TRAVELLING WITHOUT MOVING
'Virtual Insanity', 'Cosmic Girl'

SYNKRONIZED
'Canned Heat', 'Black Capricorn Day'

STATISTICS

DATE OF BIRTH
27 March 1962

PLACE OF BIRTH
London, England

INFLUENCES
Reggae music, Sly'n'Robbie, Incognito, Hi Tension and jazz rock drummer Billy Cobham

FIRST HIT
'Space Cowboy'

HIGHEST CHART POSITION
'Deeper Underground '– #1– 1998

INSTRUMENTS USED
Sonor drums and Zildjian cymbals

IN THE STYLE OF...

Jamiroquai's music is some of the grooviest, funkiest music you'll hear on Planet Earth – it's impossible not to move your feet when you hear the Jamiroquai beat. And that's down to Derrick's infectious grooves. As with most top drummers, he keeps his beats simple and goes with the music, and because his music is dance, his beats are dance. So we're going to learn how to dance – well, at least how to play it to make other people dance! Two of Derrick's best beats are what we call the four-on-the-floor bass drum, and the off-beat hi-hat, known by many as the pea-soup (because that's the sound it makes).

HOW TO PLAY LIKE DERRICK McKENZIE

In the first example, we'll look at Derrick's standard disco groove – he plays the bass drum on every beat of the bar (in other words on the 1, 2, 3 and 4) The snare drum comes on the '2' and '4' as with a normal backbeat, and the hi-hats are normal closed quavers. When you first play this try it without the snare drum, so it's just the 8s on the hi-hat and 4s on the bass drum, then bring the snare in. Now we'll try the off-beat hi-hat (pea-soup). The snare and the bass drum stay the same, and we keep playing quavers on the hi-hat. But to get Derrick's off-beat we have to open and close the hi-hats while we strike them. The easiest way to do this is lift your hi-hat foot up and down at the same time as your bass drum foot goes up and down. You'll know you're doing it right when it sounds like you're going 'pea-soup pea-soup pea-soup pea-soup'… seriously!

TRUE STORY

When he plays live with Jamiroquai Derrick sits on a 'bum-busting' stool, which is basically a drum stool with a speaker attached to it. The speaker vibrates the seat every time he kicks the bass drum, so that he can feel the beat pounding through his body. Sounds great fun, but what does it feel like when he plays after a curry…?

TRACK 44

TRACK 45

CAROLINE CORR

There's one thing for sure, you cannot ignore, Caroline Corr. One of the sweetest drummers in the business, Caroline really knows how to whack a drum when she sees it. She also plays piano for the Corrs, and is pretty nifty with the bodhran: an Irish frame drum held in the left hand and played with a little double-beaded stick in the right hand. The Corrs consist of Caroline and her two sisters, Andrea and Sharon, who along with brother Jim have become one of the biggest bands to come out of Ireland since U2. They blend traditional Irish sounds with sweet pop melodies and when they sing in harmony together it's heaven!

LISTEN TO
UNPLUGGED
'Only When I Sleep', 'Listen To The Radio', 'So Young', 'Toss The Feathers'

STATISTICS

DATE OF BIRTH
17 March 1973

PLACE OF BIRTH
Dundalk, Co. Louth, Ireland

INFLUENCES
Genesis, Prince, The Police and drummers Cindy Blackman and Sheila E

FIRST HIT
'Dreams'

HIGHEST CHART POSITION
'Breathless' – #1 – 2000

INSTRUMENTS USED
Yamaha drums and Zildjian cymbals

IN THE STYLE OF...

Since the family first started playing in Ireland in the middle of the '90s The Corrs have become so big that they've turned into what's known as a stadium band, and Caroline has had to adapt to what's known as stadium drumming – basically big, loud and simple – with strong bass drums and backbeats. Her style is very physical, and she really moves her arms up and down in a very powerful way, so she's very fit. If you want to play like Caroline you'd better do some exercises!

HOW TO PLAY LIKE CAROLINE CORR

The first thing you need to do is get fit, and play your grooves hard and tight… Caroline plays a lot of 16s on hi-hat with her grooves. So for this lesson we'll basically take Lesson 10 (the rhythm with grace notes), and use 16s on the hi-hat instead. Zoiks! But you don't have to play too fast, so don't worry… When Caroline plays, the grace notes aren't normally any quieter than the backbeat, which gives the grooves their power. But the difficult thing about this is you'll need to bring the left hand off the hats for the grace notes and the right hand off for the backbeat. So to start with, just practise the 16s with the backbeat, then the 16s with the grace notes, and then put them together. Good luck! And if you want to play a sound like the bodhran, you can play 16s rhythms on your floor tom-tom – just put a few accents in when you feel like it.

TRACK 46

CD

RINGO STARR

Starr by name and star by nature, Ringo is probably the most famous drummer on the planet – more drummers drum because of him than anyone else. When The Beatles first performed on television in the '60s to audiences of adoring and screaming fans, with Ringo shaking his head and beating his drums at the back, thousands of young dudes around the globe decided to pick up sticks and have a bash. He was also the lead singer for some tracks, like 'Yellow Submarine,' and even had his own hit singles after the Beatles split up. Plus he acted in a number of films, and if you ever watched *Thomas The Tank Engine* when you were younger, you've heard him speak, as he was the narrator for all the videos. So without a doubt, Ringo is definitely a humungous Starr…

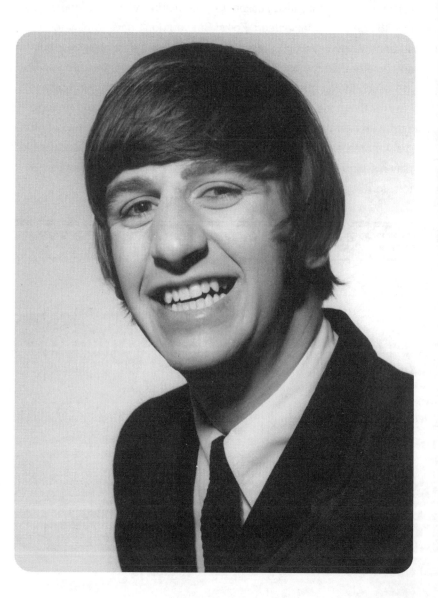

STATISTICS

DATE OF BIRTH
7 July 1940

PLACE OF BIRTH
9 Madryn Street, Liverpool

INFLUENCES
Bill Haley And The Comets, Eddie Cochran, The Four Aces, Johnnie Ray, Lonnie Donegan And The Vipers

FIRST HIT
'Please Please Me'

HIGHEST CHART POSITION
#1 (17 times in the UK singles chart – a Guinness world record)

INSTRUMENTS USED
Ludwig drums and Zildjian cymbals

LISTEN TO

THE BEATLES 1
'Ticket To Ride', 'She Loves You', 'Help', 'All You Need Is Love'

PLEASE PLEASE ME
'Please Please Me', 'I Saw Her Standing There', 'Twist And Shout'

IN THE STYLE OF...

Ringo is probably one of the most underrated drummers of all time. He might be the most famous, but people who know nothing about drums often make jokes about him being a hopeless drummer – that's just rubbish. He never played anything flash, but his style was perfect for the band's music, making it really bounce and giving it the energy it needed to make people scream! And on some songs, like 'Ticket To Ride' and 'Tomorrow Never Knows', he played new and original beats that no one had ever done before. Plus he had a great knack of drumming with the song, as he did on things like 'Please Please Me' and 'A Hard Day's Night', with his splashy hi-hats and bouncing double snare beats.

HOW TO PLAY LIKE RINGO STARR

Well, the first thing is to sit nice and high – Ringo always had his drums quite low and his stool quite high. And then while you're playing, you have to shake your head and grin – that was one of the Beatles's trademarks! When he plays a beat Ringo doesn't 'lay into' the drums, he just lets his wrists do the work His right hand swishes from side to side across the hi-hats and ride cymbal His cymbal sound is very washy, his hi-hats are virtually always slightly open so they sizzle, and sometimes he just plays his 8s on the crash cymbal When he plays a fill-in it often goes with the melody, so in the example we'll play three bars and then a simple fill with the music.

TRACK 47

TRUE STORY

When the Beatles broke up in 1970 Ringo carried on as a solo artist. He had seven Top 10 hits in the USA, including two #1s, and four in the UK. He still makes music, and has his own band, the All-Starr band, who tour every now and again in the USA. When he's singing he often has other famous drummers playing the kit, like Jim Keltner, Simon Kirke and even his son, Zak Starkey (Starkey is Ringo's real surname). Zak is a famous drummer in his own right, and has played with The Who for many years, another band that made great music in the '60s.

SUPERSTAR TIP

Whenever Ringo was asked about drumming, he always said the most important thing for a drummer is to know his or her role in the band. The drummer's job is to play the beat so the rest of the band can have freedom to play over the drums. And that's exactly what he did for the biggest band of all time!

CHAD SMITH

Buf bam bif, it's Mr Chad Smith. Chad's been banging out the beats for the one and only Red Hot Chili Peppers for nearly 20 years, and in that time he's seen them go from the hard funk thrashing of the '80s to the melodic rock of the 21st Century. He started drumming on ice cream cartons when he was seven, and once he had real drums learned to drum by playing along to his favourite records. A massive character and personality, Chad is renowned for his hard-hitting grooves, baseball hats and big cheshire cat grin. His partner-in-time is bass player Flea, and between them they are one of the funkiest rhythm sections (drums and bass) in the world today.

LISTEN TO

BLOOD SEX SUGAR MAGIK
'Give It Away', 'Under The Bridge'

BY THE WAY
'Universally Speaking', 'Throw Away Your Television'

STATISTICS

DATE OF BIRTH
25 October 1962

PLACE OF BIRTH
Minnesota, USA

INFLUENCES
Ringo Starr, Buddy Rich, Led Zeppelin, Jimi Hendrix Experience, Rush, The Doors

FIRST HIT
'Taste The Pain'

HIGHEST CHART POSITION
'By The Way' – #2 – 2002

INSTRUMENTS USED
Pearl drums and Sabian cymbals

IN THE STYLE OF...

The year 2002 saw the Chili Peppers become one of the biggest bands on the planet when they released their album *By The Way*. It stayed in the charts for over a year and has a wide selection of Chad's different styles, from the laid back ballad playing of 'I Could Die For You' to the hard funk of 'Can't Stop', and from the dynamic pounding of the title track to the driving power of 'Universally Speaking'. This last is a great example of how Chad can take a well-known simple groove and use it to drive a song from start to finish.

HOW TO PLAY LIKE CHAD SMITH

Well the first thing to do is put on a great big smile – Chad has to be one of the happiest drummers around. And if you really want to complete the effect, put on a backwards baseball cap, Chad's trademark headgear! In general Chad plays the drums hard, and his hi-hats are often very slightly open, giving a chunkier sound. To do this, you need to have your foot on the hi-hat pedal, but not pushing down. Experiment a bit to find how much pressure you need. Many of Chad's beats have quite complicated bass drum parts to go with Flea's bass lines, but sometimes he just sits back and plays a well-known rhythm, like a motown groove (motown being pop music made in the '60s and '70s by black American artists like Stevie Wonder, Marvin Gaye, and The Temptations). The most important difference between this and the beats we learned in our lessons is that the snare drum plays on every beat, ie the '1, 2, 3, and 4'. The bass drum pattern is also new with a beat in-between the '3' and '4' – listen to the CD and you should be able to get it...

TRACK 48 CD

TRUE STORY

Chad often performs on his own at what are known as drum clinics – shows that have famous drummers playing and talking about their style. At one of them Chad once said he'd give his drum kit to the first person to get up and dance in the nude. Immediately after there was a stampede of naked people rushing to the front of the stage...!

LARRY MULLEN

Without a doubt one of the most original drummers of the last 25 years, Larry Mullen plays with the most original band of the last two decades – the mighty U2. Larry, along with bassist Adam Clayton, guitarist The Edge and singer Bono, grew up in Ireland, and together have been touring the world since the early '80s, playing to massive sell-out crowds of adoring fans wherever they go. Unusually for a drummer, Larry's the quiet one of the band – most of us like to make a racket with or without drums – he just gets on with providing creative and inspiring beats for the rest of the band to weave their magic over. His early musical education began by playing in marching bands, and his military style approach to beats and fill-ins are a major part of the band's music.

LISTEN TO

WAR
'Sunday Bloody Sunday', 'New Year's Day', 'Two Hearts Beat As One'

ALL THAT YOU CAN'T LEAVE BEHIND
'Beautiful Day', 'Walk On', 'Kite'

STATISTICS

DATE OF BIRTH
31 October 1961

PLACE OF BIRTH
Dublin, Ireland

INFLUENCES
The Sweet, T-Rex, Slade, Roxy Music, David Bowie and, of course, marching bands

FIRST HIT
'Fire'

HIGHEST CHART POSITION
1 (4 times - 'Desire', 'The Fly', 'Discotheque', 'Beautiful Day')

INSTRUMENTS USED
Yamaha drums and Paiste cymbals

IN THE STYLE OF...

TRUE STORY

It was Larry who originally got U2 together. In 1976 he put a 'Musicians Wanted' message on the notice board at school, and amongst those who answered were Adam Clayton, The Edge and Bono. At first the band used to rehearse in Larry's parents' kitchen using borrowed equipment, and playing songs by bands like the Rolling Stones. Now, more than 25 years later, the band still has the same line-up and they're still giving us some of the best music ever – thanks Larry!

When U2 first arrived on the music scene, Larry Mullen's style was unique. As he himself said, because his early drumming years were spent playing snare drum in a marching band, he never really learned how to use his bass drum. In many of U2's early songs the bass drum is relatively simple, just playing 4s or even 8s thoughout the song. So to make the rhythms interesting he'd do unusual patterns between the hi-hat and the snare drum, and this is what gave him his sound.

HOW TO PLAY LIKE LARRY MULLEN

Larry comes from a marching band background, which is basically playing snare drum patterns, so practise your rudiments if you want to sound like him. Many of his early U2 beats are like marching beats, done with 16s on the hi-hat, and coming off to play the snare We'll try a classic Larry beat, with bass drum playing throughout on the '1, 2, 3, 4, etc'. Try it at first with just the bass drum and 16s on the hi-hat before you start hitting the snare drum as well. The 16s are played hand to hand (right left right left etc.), and it is always the right hand on the snare drum first. Be careful when you repeat the bars – you get four semi-quavers on the snare drum, which feels strange, but sounds great.

TRACK 49

MEG WHITE

She's all things bright, she's more than alright, she's the lovely Meg White! And Meg's band, The White Stripes, which she plays in with guitar-swinging Jack White, are just about the coolest band on the planet right now. The White Stripes are so unique there's only two of them – Meg's grooves are so beautiful they don't even bother with a bass player. She provides the perfect backing for Jack's manic guitar and vocals, and even sings some of the songs herself. Watching Meg drum is an amazing experience – she plays like she's in a trance, almost stroking the drums and cymbals with her sticks. This lady is definitely in the zone when she makes music.

LISTEN TO

WHITE BLOOD CELLS
'Hotel Yorba', 'Fell In Love With A Girl', 'Little Room'

ELEPHANT
'Seven Nation Army', 'Hardest Button To Button'

STATISTICS

DATE OF BIRTH
10 December 1974

PLACE OF BIRTH
Michigan, USA

INFLUENCES
Bob Dylan, Led Zeppelin, The Pixies, American folk music and the blues

FIRST HIT
'Hotel Yorba'

HIGHEST CHART POSITION
'Seven Nation Army' – # 5 – 2003

INSTRUMENTS USED
Ludwig and Pearl drums and Paiste cymbals

IN THE STYLE OF...

Meg White's style is sparse yet absolutely perfect for the band's music – her beats are really strong and follow the guitar riffs. Often, because there's no bass guitar in the band, she fills up the sound with splashy hi-hats and cymbals, and sometimes uses bass drum and tom-toms to give the music its depth. Meg uses a very basic set-up (four drums, two cymbals and hi-hat), and when she plays she sweeps her arms and sticks back and forth over the drums like she's brushing them.

HOW TO PLAY LIKE MEG WHITE

A lot of Meg's beats are like those we learned in the lessons, but done on toms or crash cymbal instead of hi-hat. So to start sounding like Meg try some beats on your toms and cymbal. For our Meg-style beat we're going to look at something else Meg does – 'play the riff' – which basically means she plays a beat that goes with the rhythm of the guitar. The first thing to do is open the hi-hats – not completely open, they need to be touching, but only just, so that when you play them they sound sizzly. The rhythm is played so that the only beat you hear is '1', '2' and '4' – there's no beat on the '3'. There's a crash cymbal and bass drum on the '1' and the other beats are on the snare and hi-hats. Apart from stops in the music, Meg often plays beats like this the whole way through a song with no changes or fill-ins, and it sounds fantastic!

BUDDY RICH

Rich in technique, Rich in style, Rich in feel, Rich in speed, Rich in dynamics. Basically, this guy is Buddy Rich in everything! Seriously, he may have played jazz, but ask virtually any famous drummer 'who's the greatest drummer of all time?' and they'll tell you it's Buddy Rich. In the olden days (before 1970!) he played with the greats of that time – people like Frank Sinatra, Louis Armstrong, Count Basie, Nat King Cole, Ella Fitzgerald, Miles Davis, Duke Ellington, in fact all the biggest names from jazz. And he had his own band, The Buddy Rich Big Band, that played big band jazz (well, what else did you think it was going to play?). Sadly for the music world he died in 1987 but he'll always be remembered as 'The greatest drummer in the world…ever!'

STATISTICS

DATE OF BIRTH
30 September 1917

PLACE OF BIRTH
Brooklyn, New York, USA

INFLUENCES
Count Basie Orchestra, the Benny Goodman Band, and drummers Gene Krupa, Chick Webb and Jo Jones

FIRST HIT
Buddy's hits were around before the days of charts

HIGHEST CHART POSITION
But he's #1 in our drummers chart!

INSTRUMENTS USED
Rogers, Ludwig and Slingerland drums, Zildjian cymbals

LISTEN TO

Loads of Buddy Rich stuff is no longer available, but here's some cool albums that have been put on CD: *BIG SWING FACE, THE COLLECTION: RAGS TO RICHES, SWINGIN' NEW BAND, KRUPA AND RICH*

IN THE STYLE OF...

Check this out drumsters – I have evidence that Buddy Rich is the greatest drummer ever in the history of the known universe. When I was a young drumster myself I was lucky enough to see Buddy Rich in concert, and I have to say to this day it was the most amazing drumming I've ever seen. He played so darn fast and did things with his hands and feet that I'd think were impossible if I hadn't seen them with my own eyes. He could play the fastest drum roll ever – with just one hand – I kid you not! And he was so important in music that his band really was his band – The Buddy Rich Big Band. Respect is due...

HOW TO PLAY LIKE BUDDY RICH

Are you serious? No one can play like Buddy! But we can learn the basic parts of a jazz beat like the ones Buddy played. Well, it's a start! The main difference between a basic jazz beat and a rock or pop beat is the part played on the hi-hat and ride cymbal. In jazz they don't play a straight pattern, they break it up to create what is called the 'swing'. Now it's easier on the ride (the first example), but on the hi-hat jazz players open and close the hats while they're playing, so it goes 'tsss ch ch tsss ch ch tsss' and so on, opening the hats on the '1' and '3' bass drum part – (that's the little umbrella sign in the second example) Finally, we add the swing – basically, we play the 'and' a little later than it's written in the music. Listen to the CD and I'll play you what I mean.

JAZZ ON RIDE CYMBAL

JAZZ ON HI-HATS

TRACK 51

TRACK 52

TRAVIS BARKER

He's a prankster and larker, he's the great Travis Barker. Travis joined Blink 182 after he filled in with them for a gig, learning 21 songs just a few hours before the show. The first Blink album he played on, *Enema Of The State,* sold 7,000,000 copies, and the follow up, *Take Off Your Pants And Jacket,* sold 5,000,000. Phew! Travis started playing when he was only four years old and when he was in High School he played in the school jazz group and marching band. As well as Blink 182, he has two other bands, Transplants and Boxcar Racer, and also does what are called sessions, playing drums for other pop stars' albums – he's played for the Black Eyed Peas and is the drummer on 'Trouble' by Pink.

LISTEN TO

ENEMA OF THE STATE
'Dumpweed', 'Aliens Exist'

TAKE OFF YOUR PANTS AND JACKET
'Anthem Part Two', 'Online Songs', 'The Rock Show'

STATISTICS

DATE OF BIRTH
14 November 1975

PLACE OF BIRTH
Fontana, California, USA

INFLUENCES
Stewart Copeland from The Police, Fugazi, playing in marching bands and famous drummers Steve Gadd and Dennis Chambers

FIRST HIT
'What's My Age Again?'

HIGHEST CHART POSITION
'All The Small Things' – # 2 – 2000

INSTRUMENTS USED
Orange County drums and Zildjian cymbals

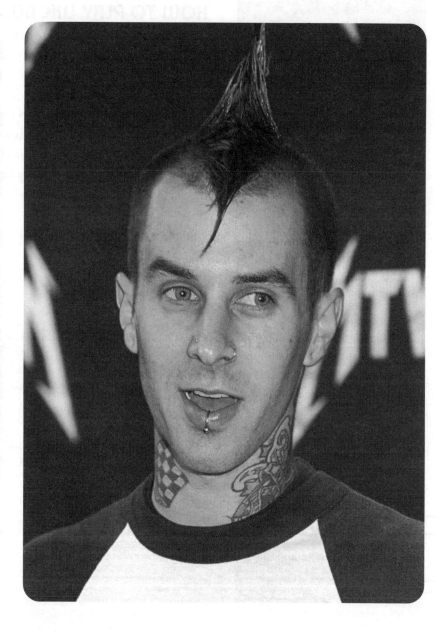

IN THE STYLE OF...

TRUE STORY

Travis is a total skateboarding dude. He was so into skateboarding that he virtually gave up drumming between the age of 11 and 15 to skate, and nowadays he runs his own clothing company, Famous Stars And Straps. The company designs and sells belt buckles and T-shirts to skater dudes and dudettes. And his other hobby is collecting cadillacs (American cars) – he owns nine of them, and has Cadillac tattoed down his side! Travis sure is one radical dude!

Although the music Blink 182 play is punk, Travis is probably the most technical player in this book (apart from Buddy Rich of course), and that means he can play more complicated beats and patterns than anyone else – and at twice the speed. Part of that is due to his spending his early years doing marching band drumming – that's playing and practising rudiments at breakneck speed. To play like Travis would take years and years of practice, but fortunately not everything he does is impossible, and we can learn one of his basic tricks, using single-stroke drum rolls instead of the backbeat '4' to get us started.

HOW TO PLAY LIKE TRAVIS BARKER

A lot of Travis's drumming is very complicated stuff, and very, very fast – zoiks! So start practising slowly, and try getting quicker! He uses a lot of what I call machine gun fills as part of his beats, little drum rolls instead of a backbeat sometimes. In our example here we play an ordinary beat for the first three bars and then in the fourth we play a roll on the toms instead of a snare on the '4' of the backbeat. To do this we need to play our right hand on the ride cymbal, and come off the ride to play the roll on the '4' The roll is basically 16s, (just four strikes), and ends with a crash cymbal and bass drum on the first beat of the next bar, as you can hear on the CD.

TRACK 53 CD

NOTES

NOTES

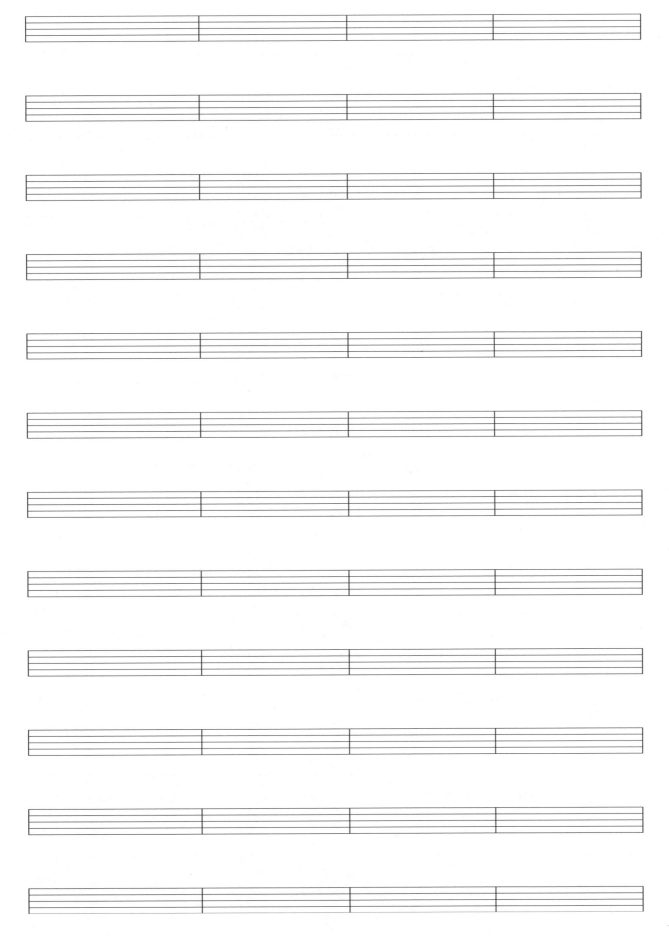

NOTES

NOTES

NOTES

GLOSSARY

4S, 8S AND 16S
Drummers use various expressions to describe different kinds of beats and parts, and 4s, 8s and 16s are what we use to describe hi-hat patterns. 4s are basically crotchets, 8s are quavers, and 16s are semi-quavers.

BACKBEAT
The backbeat is basically an expression used to describe the '2' and '4' of the snare drum in a rhythm. Most modern music, from the rock of Nirvana to the pop of Britney has a backbeat, and is an essential ingredient of most hits, so don't you forget it!

CO-ORDINATION
Getting our hands and feet to do different things at the same time.

CROTCHET
A musical note.

DYNAMICS
The word dynamic in music basically refers to the volume you are playing at – eg loud or quiet. Playing with dynamics is very important for drummers.

FILL-IN
A fill-in is a break in a beat, something we can use to take us into another beat or section of a song.

GRACE NOTES
These are quieter strikes on our snare drum that are played in-between the '2' and '4' backbeat.

GHOST NOTES
The expression some drummers use to describe grace notes. They are basically the same but just a little bit scarier… boom boom!

GROOVE
A groove is another name for a beat or rhythm. A cool groove is a cool beat, a funky groove is a funky beat, and a heavy groove is… okay, you've got it. So drummers play grooves, and when they're 'in the groove' it's a beautiful thing – groovy, man!

OPEN AND CLOSED HI-HATS
An open hi-hat is one where the cymbals are apart and the foot is loose on the pedal, a closed hi-hat is one where the cymbals are tight together and the foot is pressing down on the pedal.

PATTERNS AND PARTS
These are the rhythms you hit on the bits of your kit. When you put the patterns or parts together you end up with a beat. Ker-ching!

QUAVER
Musical note.

RHYTHM SECTION
The bass player and drummer in a group are known as this.

SEMI-QUAVER
Musical note.

STAVE
Lines that music is written on.

STICKING
In drumming this means which stick we're using – the stick held in the left hand or the one in the right hand. In real life it means gluing things together… boom boom!

TUBS
Another word for drums. So tub thumping means drumming.

VERSE, BRIDGE AND CHORUS
These are the main parts of a song. The verse is the bit with lots of words that often starts a song, the chorus is the sing-along bit that repeats several times, and the bridge is the bit that links the verse and the chorus.

ANSWERS TO TEST QUESTIONS

LESSON 1: ARE YOU SITTING COMFORTABLY?

1. Your right foot should be on the bass drum pedal and your left foot on the hi-hat pedal.
2. You hold it a third of the way up from the butt end, between the thumb and the forefinger, with the other fingers curled underneath around the stick, and the hands slightly turned (Or something to that effect!).
3. Shoulders, arms and wrists.
4. To protect our hearing – drums are LOUD!

LESSON 2: HOW TO READ DRUM MUSIC

1. Stave.
2. Bottom space (And no, it's not because the bass drum is like a big bottom).
3. Four.
4. Four quavers (twice as fast as four crotchets).

LESSON 3: THE BASIC BEAT

1. Left hand plays the snare drum, right hand plays the hi-hats
2. Whichever you find more comfortable.
3. These are the different rhythms you hit on the bits of your kit. When you put the patterns or parts together you end up with a beat. (TIP – If you haven't read the glossary yet, this is the time to look. It's where we learn the meaning of words and expressions we don't know.)
4. Play along to your favourite tapes and CDs – it is probably best to wear headphones when you do this.

LESSON 4: XTRA BASS DRUM BEATS

1. The Backbeat.
2. Two.
3. Slow down.
4. A slight difference can be really weird – but don't worry, at least you can't be kissed by your drum kit…

LESSON 5: XTRA SNARE DRUM BEATS

1. In the middle or the bell.
2. Oooh yes indeed!
3. Tribal.
4. What's the answer? I don't know, just see how many you can come up with. Don't forget you can use the ride cymbal or tom-tom as well as the hi-hat.

LESSON 6: DIFFERENT STROKE FOR DIFFERENT FOLKS

1. 4s.
2. 16s.
3. Yo Punk, we use it for punk.
4. The right – is that alright?

LESSON 7: OPENING AND CLOSING THE HI-HATS

1. An open hi-hat has the cymbals apart and the foot loose, a closed hi-hat has the cymbals together and the foot pressed down
2. With the right and left feet going up and down alternately on the pedals
3. On the 'and' before the '2' and the '4'.
4. Oooooh yes indeedy!

LESSON 8: FILL-INS, RUDIMENTS AND ACCENTS

1. A rudiment is a type of pattern played with the sticks, with the hands doing co-ordinated movements.
2. Single-stroke roll, double-stroke roll, paradiddle, three-stroke ruff.
3. Paradiddle.
4. With the accent on the first beat.

LESSON 9: BEATS WITH FILL-INS

1. Second space from the bottom.
2. Crash cymbal (and bass drum).
3. No.
4. It doesn't matter too much which one you hit.

LESSON 10: GRACE NOTES

1. Single-stroke roll.
2. Quieter strikes on our snare drum that are played in-between the '2' and '4' backbeat.
3. 'We Will Rock You'.
4. Well, it wasn't me…